National and International Acclaim
for *Emotional Language* from Readers Like You

"In this succinct and poignant treatise, Zaki Huq sheds valuable light on ways to enhance our communication, improve our relationships and be more effective in our personal and professional endeavors. By focusing on our senses, and through the employment of worthy self-reflective exercises, Huq guides the reader towards a path of fostering greater connections with humanity and the world around us."

—Eric Katz, M.A., Law and Diplomacy
High school teacher
New York

"*Emotional Language* is a must read for all. Zaki Huq goes straight to the source of the human experience and extracts the knowledge that is so needed in our current paradigm. This handbook offers a template that helps us connect the dots between what we "think" we are and how we are actually expressing ourselves in our daily lives. This book will bridge these gaps, showing us how to thrive in our human relationships."

—Brendon McKeon, CPC
Director, The OneBEing Project
San Isidro, Costa Rica

"Mr. Huq uses rich language and vivid descriptive passages in this easy-to-read handbook. This thought-provoking book challenges what you think you know about yourself and at the same time expresses ideas so effortlessly that you find yourself wondering if you knew them all along. Mr. Huq's writing is infused with vivid real-life examples of when he has used Emotional Language and practical exercises that you can't wait to complete."

—Petal Jaffrey, M.A. Counseling Psychology
Child Therapist
Geneva, Switzerland

"I met Mr. Huq over twenty years ago as he began working with high-risk and challenged youth. As a juvenile justice professional, I was intrigued by his non-threatening approach to communication and creating change in others. Through his extensive research and vast experience, Mr. Huq has contributed an indispensable resource in this handbook that we can all add to our "toolkit". When implementing a training program for social work or justice personnel, this is a must-read for your staff."

—*Paul Medlyn*
Juvenile Probation Supervisor
Arizona

"A moving and sincere book, *Emotional Language* is both interactive and practical. As a former teacher in the German public schools for over thirty-five years, I see its everyday relevance as a resource for teachers. It provides many opportunities for educators to explore with their students the essence of communication and the different ways barriers can be removed to cultivate greater reciprocity, equality, and empathy between people."

—*Carl Gerdes*
Retired teacher
Frankfurt, Germany

"*Emotional Language* is a valuable resource that can be applied equally to differences of nationality, language, skill level, or economic level. A non-judgmental awareness of difference and the ability to adapt to it is what determines success or failure in communication. It is essential for persons in positions of authority over vulnerable populations to understand a client's perspective if there is any hope of changing behaviors."

—*Myrl Weaver*
Corrections Officer
Washington State Department of Corrections

"This handbook fills the void in formal education and training for social work professionals in nonverbal communication. It significantly enriches the field by expanding the tools available for direct practitioners. Mr. Huq's work is a critical guide for learning to live and work effectively in our society."

—*Helen Dombalis, MSW, MPH*
Social worker
Washington, DC

"Through diligent adherence to practicing his clear and undeniable ideas about who our children are and how they make it from day to day, Zaki was able to bring the concepts of friendship, shared experiences and accomplishment into Dylan's life. His insightful methods work. Now living independently, something we believed impossible, Dylan took his first steps under the guidance of Zaki."

—*Kevin and Dotty Hoyle*
Parents of a young adult with autism
North Carolina

"Beautifully written in clear and elegantly simple terms, *Emotional Language* explains how we can connect and communicate with others despite our differences. This handbook is particularly helpful for people volunteering in communities that are different from their own."

—*Mary Morrison, M.S., Adult Education*
Director
The Kernodle Center for Service Learning and Community Engagement
Elon University, North Carolina

"From my personal encounters with intercultural communication within my parish as well as international NGOs, I deeply share Huq's conviction that we must go beyond spoken words in order to better understand one another. This comprehensive framework for using Emotional Language opens the door to a new path for us all."

—*Steffen Rottler*
Pastor
Bern, Switzerland

"In this informative handbook Mr. Huq gives clear insight into true holistic communication. He asks us to be completely attentive to our moments with each other. By being alert and present to interactive cues, we open the door to vibrant discovery with each other. With careful watchfulness of personal perceptions we can actually bridge the gap that may separate us. Mr. Huq beckons us to a sensitivity that dispels fear and invites compassion and understanding. Teachers, counselors, indeed all of us, would be served to heed his message and practice the clear guidance from this handbook."

—*Jack Staudacher*
Educator and Holistic Health Therapist
Arizona

"Whatever your level of communication skill, *Emotional Language* offers a common sense approach backed by decades of active observation and practical application. Mr. Huq's insights from his extensive experience working with individuals and groups from diverse backgrounds have been distilled brilliantly into this readable, original, and seminal book."

—*J Wong*
Managing Director, JMW Resources
Paris, France

"I wholeheartedly endorse this work and appreciate how it leads the reader to introspection and engages us in a unique conversation. Huq plants thought-provoking ideas that push the current paradigm of effective communication."

—*Joseph Carr, M.Ed, QMHP*
Secondary Education Teacher
Oregon

Mary,
Please accept this book as a small
token of appreciation. It represents
a vision for the world I believe
you and I share.
Your support was crucial for
making this book a reality.
Thank you,
Zaki

emotional language

The Art and Science of
Communication for Human Development

ZAKI HUQ

Copyright © 2011 by Zaki Huq

All rights reserved. No part of this handbook may be reproduced in any form or by any means, graphic, electronic or mechanical, including photocopying, recording, taping or by any information storage and retrieval system without the written permission of the author.

Emotional Language handbook and consulting services
can be purchased at
www.emotionallanguage.org

First Edition 2011
Author photograph, cover, and book design by Jason Smith
ISBN: 978-0-615-41565-9
Printed in the United States of America

CONTENTS

ACKNOWLEDGMENTS

The conception of Emotional Language was generated by time spent with countless individuals throughout my life. I am grateful to them all for provoking my thinking and sharing their lives with me. Special thanks are extended to Akhlaque, Bear, Charles, Charlotte, Cheryl, Dale, Dana, Darlene, Dylan, Hannibal, Jane, Jesse, Kojo, Mara, Mason, Nancy, Nicole, Reza, Sagar, Stan, and Swapan.

My deep appreciation goes to Martica Bacallao, Joe Carr, Carissa Cascio, Helen Dombalis, Carl Gerdes, Kevin and Dotty Hoyle, Petal Jaffrey, Eric Katz, Steve May, Brendon McKeon, Paul Medlyn, Mary Morrison, Stephen Rottler, Jack Staudacher, Myrl Weaver, and James Wong for their professional expertise and generosity of time in reviewing this handbook.

My heartfelt gratitude is extended to Shirley Colagrossi and Gray Brunk for their generous feedback and support for my ideas. I am indebted to Julie Fann and Jenny Huq for their thoughtful and skilled editing.

My strength to live with conviction and compassion is deeply rooted in my parents, Brenda and Momin, and my sisters, Farida and Atya. My devotion to them will always withstand time and distance.

I am especially grateful for my partner and confidant, Jenny, and our two sons, Durante and Amadeo, for enduring my continuous observation of their emotional expressions. They are my sail, compass, and anchor in my journey of endless discoveries. My love for them is eternal.

PREFACE

Language facilitates human development; through language, people communicate experiences and connect with others. When we think of language, we think of words, but there is something more basic and innate embedded in all languages that is not quite apparent at first.

You could say that for the first thirty years of my life I listened more than I spoke. At first, I had no choice. When I was a child, my parents spoke to each other in a language that was different from the one they spoke with me. Now I am almost fifty, and most of my working life has involved understanding and representing individuals who, for many reasons, did not or could not explain their fears or needs through words. My ability to communicate with—and on behalf of—them grew from my childhood and my travels; I gravitated towards people and countries whose verbal language was unfamiliar to me. In these settings, I realized that communication precedes speech; *what comes before we speak* matters most. When I could not understand the words, I began to grasp the language, the language of emotion, which I now call Emotional Language.

The purpose of this handbook is two-fold. First, it will reacquaint you with your Emotional Language and demonstrate why it is integral to your everyday communication and understanding. The material and its presentation are designed for you to easily understand and integrate Emotional Language into your professional and personal lives. Secondly, having personally experienced a void in education and training to prepare human services professionals, teachers, caregivers, volunteers, and parents for effective service and care, I offer this handbook in an effort to drive the development of Emotional Language competencies. When we become literate in Emotional Language, we become empowered to meet each other's individual needs.

In Emotional Language, nothing is insignificant and everything matters. This subject is at the core of any healthy, interpersonal relationship. Developing the skill to interpret or translate Emotional Language gives us the essential tools to connect with one another. You will realize the depth and importance of this subject as you begin to apply the lessons from this handbook.

Each chapter shows *what* you can learn from your senses and *how* this knowledge can be evaluated and employed. As your understanding of Emotional Language grows, so will your confidence and competence. To facilitate your fluency, engaging and reflective exercises are included. Please note: if you are reading a digital version you will need pen and paper to complete the exercises.

I begin this handbook with the story of my journey, *On Becoming Fluent*. It communicates how I came to understand and appreciate the value and universal nature of Emotional Language. Chapter two introduces the critical elements of the philosophical art that influence the depth of understanding and how you apply Emotional Language in your daily communication. Chapter three focuses on the two fundamental experiences that affect communication, insecurity and security, and the way they are expressed biologically. Included is an identifiable and practical compilation of emotional expressions, organized by corresponding sections of the body. Chapter four covers the critically important issues of power and ethics when engaging in Emotional Language. Chapter five discusses the science behind Emotional Language, describing the biological process of an experience as it affects your body and how it is expressed. The final chapter analyzes four case studies to underscore the significant elements at play within an experience as they pertain to the application of Emotional Language. It also suggests ways to start developing your own Emotional Language skills to use in your work and personal life.

Because you do not yet know how the following information will migrate from these pages into your everyday experiences, read patiently. Let the significance of Emotional Language unfold as you communicate with others.

—Zaki Huq
Emotional Language Consulting
emotionallanguage.org

emotional language

CHAPTER ONE

INTRODUCTION

On Becoming Fluent

The place where my home stood was literally at the crossroads of the modern and ancient world. The area was called the "Great Emptiness." To the west, the people lived in a village where time stood still and the wilderness surrounded them. It was the home of wild animals. Our house was a two-story building with bars on the windows. They were there to keep the daring monkeys out.

The red clay path that connected the villagers to the modern world was squeezed between the river and the boundary of our house. The villagers travelled by walking and on moonless nights this and all the other paths were darker than the darkest abyss. The village had a well in the center, but no electricity. The people made a living as their ancestors had done for centuries, as farmers and fisherman.

To the east, modernity reigned. Here people made a living with industrial tools and intellectual professions, and they travelled by car. This is where the diplomats lived, and beyond them the country's air force base lay. The base was off limits, but I often roamed where the foreigners lived. Their houses were big, and their night sky was illuminated by powerful street lights. I mostly saw their shadows and pieces of their appearance through their high metal gates.

My school was to the east and my playground was to the west. From the upstairs veranda, I could soak up the sunrise and sunset over both these worlds. My home and family were both the center of my universe and my gateway into whatever world I chose to be in. Living in such a juncture allowed me to weave my experiences into many discoveries, near misses, and disasters that left my parents not always amused. For me, everyday was an adventure in tropical Asia.

The time we lived in required us to understand other people's intentions and motivations through their behaviors. In the midst of war, differences in languages, religious practices, and political affiliations matter more than in times of peace. In addition, there were differences of philosophy and socioeconomics that I observed as people engaged with my family. Heightened observation was essential for my survival. Consequently, I developed an acute awareness of subtle behavioral changes and the implications of a single word within the context of public and private communication. The spoken language I grew up with did not use words for "please" or "thank you"; these courtesies were not required. Rather, these expressions of humility and gratitude were simply understood by the way in which a request was delivered or received. When two individuals moved closer to one another, they were showing emotional connection; when they moved away from one another, they were signaling an emotional distance. I observed their movements and learned to understand the meaning of their emotions.

The clouds of one war passed when I was three; however, another loomed on the horizon, finally coming to a genocidal end when I was nine. War either confines you to eternal darkness or gives you great awareness. I witnessed how humans are capable of inflicting unimaginable pain and suffering on others and what we are all capable of doing to ensure survival. I learned that war strips away frivolity and demands only the essentials.

As a child, I quickly realized life and death were two sides of the same coin. They were discussed daily at the dinner table between my father, a surgeon, and my mother, a surgical nurse, and were witnessed by my two sisters and me. Being exposed to the fusion of sickness, health, happiness, and despair of the young and the old gave me the luxury of observing human behavior at its most bare. Besides watching the fragility of life unfold, discussions at home focused on science, history, and geography as well as power and privilege.

I walked with my father on his pre and post-surgical rounds as he talked about his patients who might or might not live. Seeing him face-to-face at their bedsides intensified my desire--the desire we all have--to live, feel secure, and seek comfort. It revealed to me the power and effect we have on others by our mere presence, our acts of caring, and our genuine desire to help.

Being exposed to his work at a young age also made me understand how the distance or barriers we create can shield us from experiences that make us uncomfortable. This I learned when I was asked to take photographs of a surgical procedure. I watched my father cut into the skin and flesh of the patient through the opening in the drape that covered the patient's body. I quickly realized that having my eye pressed against the viewfinder was the best place for me. Having the patient covered afforded me comfort and detachment during this experience. As long as the human form remained altered or fragmented, I felt secure.

Equally enlightening was my weekly shopping trip into the open-air village market with my Anglo-Saxon, blue-eyed mother mingling in a sea of dark-eyed, dark-skinned East Asians who spoke a different language from her native tongue. On those days I witnessed the desire to know and understand each other and the spirit of unhindered human affection. In that market, it was not the exchange of money that made people rich but rather their genuine kindness.

My childhood was filled with emotional contrasts, in that I played with the girls and their dolls and ran with the boys and their knives. Life was inseparably tangled with death, young with old, men with women, able with the disabled, rich with the poor, and the literate with the illiterate. There was no place to hide or segregate one's emotional reactions to one another.

For me, events, cultures, and languages have spanned countries and continents, crisscrossing each other through neocolonialism, dictatorships, and democracies at a very rapid pace. These experiences taught me that sorrow and joy are universal; all groups and individuals share these feelings as well as the capacity to extend compassion. It was one act of compassion that saved my own family's life on a fateful day during the height of the war. As we stood in the hallway of our home, we were stunned that my father had somehow escaped the clutches of his executioners, covered in blood from their attempt to kill him. Suddenly a knock on the door made us all shudder and freeze in fear. "They" were at the door. The occupying force was out to exterminate the members of society, such as my father, who provided critical services. However, one man had compassion, which gave him the courage to risk his own life and step forward to provide my family safe passage. Just when we thought death was at the door, we were given a second chance at life.

My experience was not mine alone, nor was it unique. For every tragic story there was another that was even greater. Moving across the world, I have glimpsed and tasted the spectrum of the human condition and experience.

Throughout my life, I have learned not to look for words to describe pain or pleasure, as they can both leave you speechless. As a non-English speaker, at the age of sixteen I found myself in an international boarding school on an island off the coast of North Africa. In this environment, the student body and even the teachers operated in social groups dictated by their respective languages and cultures. I spoke not one of their languages. Therefore, I could not rely on a particular language or cultural cues for social acceptance. I needed survival skills of another nature that would allow me to understand and interact with my new environment.

Clarity about what it means to be accepted as part of a family and social group came later when I was living with a North American indigenous tribe. In spite of our differences, they completely embraced me, demonstrating the power of social acceptance. It was not the words I used or the gifts I bore that allowed me to enter their homes and share their lives; rather, it was the speed in which I entered their personal space and how much I valued and respected their experience that governed the interaction.

Speed creates friction and friction creates energy or heat. I observed this same phenomenon during my interaction and communication with the people of this tribe. If the speed of my communication was too rapid, I created friction and misunderstanding ensued. Exceeding the optimum speed did not allow me to remain in sync or maintain a comfortable rhythm with them. It created heat that scalded the other and brought about confusion.

I practiced synchronizing my sensory perception with the people of the tribe. I followed their lead, altering my speed—walking, not running—so as not to scald, burn, or leave one behind but to create warmth, comfort, and the desire to stay together. This pace allowed me to be more aware of the details of how we made each other feel and how my behavior impacted their individual experiences. It allowed me to understand that our perceived differences were only a temporary and superficial illusion.

Over time I discovered I was able to navigate easily and move freely within social circles by relying on my awareness of behavioral cues that expressed feelings of security and insecurity. The more diverse the social environment, the more fluid I became in my ability to navigate with confidence within the different groups. My ability to speak a verbal language was no longer a prerequisite for my social acceptance.

My fluency in nonverbal communication was tested in my first job in a European nursing home where many of the residents were no longer coherent or mentally capable of verbally articulating their needs. This exposure to physical and mental vulnerability, frailty, and dependence on others for personal well-being was intense. In the beginning, I must admit, I was unsure of my ability to connect with the residents, so I skirted around them.

What gave me the courage to get involved and not hold back was a memory of a childhood conversation with my mother. When I was ten, my mother and I were travelling back from my first of many volunteer experiences in a transitional home for families who had children with physical limitations. She asked me, "Did you notice how they all like to laugh like you?" She was gently pointing out what we had in common rather than how we were different. She was also highlighting the power of laughter which, throughout my life, has opened the doors of security for others and has allowed me intimate access into the lives of those who were mentally and physically vulnerable. It has been the master key.

Since my time in the nursing home, work has taken me across and deep inside America to diverse communities and environments covering a broad spectrum of backgrounds and ages. I have used Emotional Language to communicate with violent street gangs in California, adjudicated and abandoned children in Arizona, recent immigrants in the Northeast, Native American families in the southwest and the Dakotas, and African-American families in North Carolina. Mixed in-between were toddlers and youth of well-educated, middle class, white America; urban, adult convicts; seniors, human services employees, and volunteers.

These populations were not as different as you might suspect; they all needed to feel secure and they expressed that sense of security or insecurity through a universal language. Their emotional expressions were the same whether they were well established with secure employment and material wealth or had to beg for food with no apparent personal accomplishments to speak of besides being alive.

Working with people in challenging circumstances has not been difficult for me. I credit this to emotionally aligning my awareness with the experiences of others. As I empathize, I truly identify with their emotional expressions and needs. As a result, in my work I have not had to rely on verbal indicators of a person's feelings of security, insecurity, comfort, or discomfort.

To understand a person without speaking, I discovered I had to physically place myself in the direct line of the other person's experience. To become sensitive to the probable impact of another's experiences, I had to engage all of my senses. I had to risk and abandon my own sense of security and embrace insecurity. To overcome my instinctual defense mechanisms, I had to be relaxed. I learned that without a relaxed mental and physical state, I could not achieve what I call the *principal of uncommitted focus*.

I discovered this principal through the game of table tennis, known in America as ping pong. Because you do not know where the ball is going to be directed, you have to be prepared to go wherever the ball is sent and accommodate its need. When I tried to predetermine its destination, trajectory, velocity or reaction to my paddle, I lost the game. With uncommitted focus, however, my senses were free to adjust to the dynamic changes within the moment of impact. Being open in mind and body, my energy could fuel an internal alertness within both spheres. I became perceptive, receptive, and empowered to seize the moment.

Sensory alignment played a central role in my early work as a facilitator, when I was responsible for the integration of newly arrived Asian and African children into European culture and education. Being physically next to them in the classroom, in the cafeteria, and on the playground, I quickly discovered how alien these places and experiences were for these newcomers. To them, nothing was familiar and everything was new. Imagine finding your way around at such a young age. Could you, even now, learn the basics of a foreign education and language without the support of people you know and trust? Such a burden, born alone, is a monumental task at any age.

Watching these brave children, I began to understand that a person's initial emotional response is a more accurate indicator of an experience than a verbal response. Many individuals fear or shy away from intense emotional involvement, as if a part of them will be lost in the process. In fact, quite the opposite happens. A greater (not a lesser) awareness of self is realized when your emotions become intensely activated. During emotional expressions, we move beyond our own limitations. In doing so, we do not lose ourselves, we find ourselves in someone else. I equate this perspective to walking along the edge of a cliff. The further away you are from the edge of that cliff, the less you are able to see and appreciate the grandeur of the view.

Over the years, I have learned that understanding Emotional Language is an art form that can only be appreciated and utilized when personal inhibitions have been discarded. In my experience, war and life-threatening circumstances introduced me to expressions of security and insecurity. You may experience these expressions in environments that are less dangerous. Any environment that scares, challenges, or surprises you can be a gateway to Emotional Language.

Experiences of security, insecurity, comfort, and discomfort are felt across every continent and culture. They are felt daily in the most prosperous of western cities as well as in the most remote corners of the poorest nations. A teenager who believes he has no alternatives to gang membership, a senior who is neglected, a child whose imagination or fear is belittled, or an ill individual who is deprived of thoughtful care are all entrusted to others—be they community members, care providers, teachers, guardians, physicians, or counselors—who have the power to either offer security or create a state of war by robbing them of opportunity, love, protection, and nourishment.

I experienced this absence of thoughtful care when I suffered a sports-related injury to my neck, which temporarily compromised my ability to function mentally and physically. This debilitating experience made me realize just how vulnerable we all are at any given moment. Although my knowledge of biomechanics was gained through my experience as a wellness advisor for terminally ill and rehabilitating clients, my injury taught me the degree to which we are all dependent on a properly functioning body and how disruptions can significantly affect our perception of all that we experience. Therefore, I believe educating yourself through study and experience in the subjects of physiology and psychology is crucial for your overall effectiveness as a communicator.

In my mid-thirties I learned to walk, to truly walk, when I began to do so with a friend who was terminally ill. He was being consumed by throat and neck cancer and was no longer able to speak. We walked regularly for over one year, most of it in silence. We spoke in a language that required no words; our physical presence expressed all that we felt. We understood the value of the experience of each step we took, even though each step brought him one step closer to his death.

In my mid-forties I walked with another friend, one with autism. By accepted standards, talking and making eye contact were not his forte. Walking together, we appeared to others to be worlds apart, but nothing could have been further from the truth. Our connection was complete, and our awareness of each other was absolute, yet we were devoid of chatter.

The depth of my friend's awareness of my presence defied many assumptions about individuals with autism. He detected and discarded the slightest intrusion into our world—he was masterful. For him, there was no room in our relationship for physical or intellectual prowess. He was not preoccupied with how much I cared about him or his environment; he just knew if I didn't. He cemented my own understanding that the notion of winning or losing does not belong in any healthy relationship. He clarified how insidious and subversive the effects of glorified or misplaced power can be. This skilled individual helped me realize that Emotional Language needed to be put on paper.

Continuous talking, describing, naming, and theorizing are an obsession for many, and they seldom stop to consider whether these actions are relevant or useful. We possess a cultural tendency to fill the void of silence with words as we fill our homes with possessions. But this compulsion ends when we learn to recognize Emotional Language.

In my experience, when you are truly involved in an interaction and struck by its magnificence, you go beyond verbal conversation. When the involvement absorbs you to the point that you are inseparable from the experience, you no longer remain aware of your own physical body. This connection ultimately achieves zen, the optimal state of sensory awareness, when the depth of communication is no longer defined by age, color, gender, knowledge, or ability. Emotional Language transcends these barriers and others inherent in verbal languages.

My journey toward becoming fluent in Emotional Language continues to offer me lessons each day. Herein, I share with you my understanding of our most natural and effective form of communication.

Universal Mother Tongue

All languages allow people to come together to share their thoughts, needs, and feelings. Emotional Language is unique because it is innate; from birth, we can communicate with others through Emotional Language. This is the universal mother tongue that is everyone's first language. We learn to see, hear, taste, smell, and touch each other in ways that no verbal language can articulate. Emotional Language joins each of us. We are pieces of a puzzle made not of paper but of flesh, blood, and spirit. The spaces we each occupy through our experiences, behavior, and intellect become mutually accessible, even shared spaces, through Emotional Language. Emotional Language communicates the slightest and the deepest of experiences brushing against your body and mind; nothing escapes its awareness and no one escapes its imprint. It is not linear or subject to human control; it is spontaneous and invulnerable to subjective manipulation. It flows effortlessly at every moment through every fiber of your being. When you rediscover and understand your Emotional Language, you come together with other individuals and recognize your common human experience.

What is Emotional Language?

Emotional expressions are your primary physical response to what you experience. If you accept the premise that experiences shape your memory and your world view, then experiences play a critical role in the way you relate to people and your environment. Consequently, overlooking Emotional Language ignores who you are as an individual. No one can avoid the natural human response of expressing emotions. Emotional Language helps you recognize how an experience affects your body, understand why it is meaningful, and translate those feelings and values to others.

Successful emotional communicators acknowledge how others feel about an experience. This recognition is the most important affirmation in any relationship because conveying that the person is valued as an individual builds trust. Regrettably, the concept of Emotional Language is seldom discussed; as a consequence, it is seldom recognized and even more rarely practiced purposefully. This emotional illiteracy limits our ability to function fully.

Our species relies heavily on vision, touch, smell, taste, and hearing to detect comfort and discomfort, as well as security and insecurity. Yet societies push us daily to verbalize our experiences, rather than develop our sensory perceptions. Using words to effectively communicate our needs or express our feelings about an experience is a gradual process that requires a rich vocabulary and years of thoughtful practice to develop a mature level of proficiency. Contrary to verbal expression, Emotional Language is intrinsic and accessible.

To understand the important role that Emotional Language plays, you need to distinguish Emotional Language not only from verbal language but also from culturally dictated body language. Body language incorporates physical gestures within speech to emphasize what is being communicated. These gestures exist and evolve out of regionally-specific cultural norms. By contrast, Emotional Language is universal in its expressions and biological in nature. How emotional expressions manifest in your body and the meaning they communicate to others are vital to all human interactions. It is these emotional expressions that we will explore in detail in this handbook.

CHAPTER TWO

CRITICAL ELEMENTS
OF THE ART

This chapter introduces you to what I have learned from experience to be the critical elements that develop and purify communication into an art form. To understand the significant influence they have on communication, consider the analogy below.

Imagine a tree that has been shaped over time by an ocean breeze. You do not see the air that causes these changes, only the effects it leaves behind.

emotional language

Developing Observation Skills

During any communication, if your observation is limited to one sense or ability, then it loses its scope. Communication should not be limited to what the eyes can see, the ears can hear, or the hands can touch. The observation needs to be multi-layered and broad enough to incorporate all of your senses. The net needs to be cast far and wide.

Your ability to see, hear, touch, smell, and taste are your tools for comprehensive awareness. Each of the tools needs to be operational, engaged, and receptive to information that may surface at any time. No one tool trumps the others; instead, each relies on the other to guide and confirm. Together, this team provides the timely and accurate information that we need to understand, engage, and disengage with others appropriately.

Observing with all senses while engaged requires a high degree of tact, subtlety, and self-control. The approach cannot be blunt; nobody likes the feeling of being under the microscope. When observers are not discrete, the observed person can feel not only uncomfortable but also threatened.

Once you have mastered observation, turn your attention to interpretation. To determine the significance of observed expressions, you need to be fully aware of your own actions and expressions as well as information within the person's environment.

Vision
Even though eye contact is necessary for you to acknowledge the other person and to maintain focus and engagement, visual observation requires the opposite. It entails looking without staring or focusing and picking up information within the scope of a glance or peripheral vision.

Hearing
Listening is not just an act of being quiet; it is also the act of being aware of and engaged with the other person. If listening is limited to what is being said only in words, then what is being heard will be monotone.

To hear all that someone is expressing, you must hear every note that is played as well as those that are not. The sound of silence can be deafening.

Touch

Touching is the art of making physical contact without prodding, gripping, trapping, dominating, or violating. Gathering information through touch is in some ways similar to vision. The information is picked up within the context of physical movement and contact, such as hand shaking, deliberate touching, or lightly brushing against another. The intensity or gentleness of your grip, as well as the tension in your musculature, can communicate your sensitivity to and/or security in your current environment.

Smell

Unless the odor you emit has a strong presence, like sweat or blood, it goes unnoticed. This belies the important role it plays in influencing your communication and behavior. Odors coming from and going to you can indicate and dictate both your physical and mental state. Because odor has an invisible presence, you may underestimate the information it carries and the subtle, yet powerful, influence it has over your interactional behavior.

Taste

Taste and smell go hand-in-hand; however, being able to taste another person is not a practical or socially acceptable means of gathering information or reaching mutual understanding. Exceptions are a mother nursing a baby or physical intimacy. Nonetheless, taste does provide another means of communication. During your exploration of your new world as a child, you put edible and inedible items into your mouth to learn about your environment. As you developed, your ability to smell without having to taste helped you determine what was safe to put in your mouth.

What emotional expressions do you tend to notice during communication?

_____

_____

_____

_____

_____

_____

_____

_____

_____

_____

_____

_____

_____

_____

_____

The Art of Positioning

Imagine that you are a house that is alive, a house with many rooms and windows. Your face is the biggest room with the most windows. When it is dark outside and the lights are turned on, it is easy to see which room is being used and for what purpose. Now imagine the lights represent your outward emotional expressions. They illuminate the rooms, allowing the observer to see where you are in the house. Their brightness reveals the intensity of your experience. The brighter the light, the more overt the expression, and the easier it is for others to perceive what you are communicating.

This perception is easy when the conditions are right—if it is dark outside and if, like a house, you remain static. But what if the conditions were less favorable; what if there were competing expressions (surrounding lights rather than darkness); and what if, unlike a house, you were fluid?

- What if the observer does not know the function of each room or is too far away from the house to see the intensity of the illumination?
- What if the observer is too close and is only able to see through one window?
- What if there is no illumination?
- What if the natural light makes it difficult to see the illumination?
- What if the illumination is turned on and off constantly?
- What if the curtains are drawn and do not allow light to escape?

The art of positioning begins with an awareness and knowledge of the many ways an experience can be expressed and, therefore, communicated. Fortunately, there is more than one indicator of emotional expression. Recognizing and interpreting cues expressed through vision, hearing, touch, and smell gives you the greatest opportunity to understand the value of an experience and the expressions it creates.

Perspective alters perception.

Do you allow others to observe you?

What barriers do you construct to conceal your expressions?

_____

_____

_____

_____

_____

_____

_____

_____

_____

_____

_____

_____

_____

_____

Critical Response Time

The communication of feelings through spoken words is dependent on the speed, clarity, and accuracy of vocabulary. It is also dictated by the interpersonal relationship between individuals and the level of security the communicator possesses. Insecurity diminishes your ability to speak with precision. By the time you have asked someone to express his or her needs, let alone articulate them in a stressful situation, you have already missed the opportunity to respond effectively. In a physical injury, the caregiver's response time will determine the *value* of the care that is given. Similarly, the faster you understand how another's experience affects him or her, the more valuable your response will become. Using Emotional Language improves your critical response time.

"When" matters.

Tracking Expressions

Once you have observed an expression, be prepared for other expressions to surface from the individual. An emotional expression communicates the past (what was just experienced), the present (how it impacts the person), and signals the future (what the person is likely to do to cope with the experience). One expression will usually lead to another to either validate the initial impact or communicate the dissipation of the experience. This will allow you, as the observer, to modify your own behavior. Tracking all expressions facilitates optimum communication; one expression alone may fail to communicate the depth of an experience, but following the narrative of expressions allows you to infer the true meaning and respond adeptly.

The path is never lost when you stay on track.

Recall a time when you have adjusted your behavior based on your observation of another's expressions.

_____

_____

_____

_____

_____

_____

_____

_____

_____

_____

_____

_____

_____

_____

Distance and Empathy

Physical distance, the space between two people, includes personal space as well as the space created by obstructions. When left unattended, distance can undermine your ability to understand the depth of Emotional Language. Layer by layer, it strips away the effectiveness of your senses. While physical distance can legitimize a lack of empathy, the distance created by indifference is more brutal and psychologically manipulative than that created by physical distance.

Indifference is the absence of *empathy*; empathy is a popular term, but it is not well understood. When you enter into an interaction armed simply with the word "empathy" and its clinical meaning, a greater indifference can result. True empathy needs to be felt, and this can only happen as a result of lived experience. Empathy, the intangible art of sharing, is the key ingredient in any communication or interpersonal relationship; it allows us to understand each other's experience of joy or sorrow, pain or pleasure, rage or contentment. It permits us to see ourselves in others. It reciprocates well-being and ensures and preserves life and dignity. Empathy is the invisible mirror you carry; how well you see the reflection of yourself in others will define the depth or shallowness of your empathy. To embody empathy, you must abandon distance as well as indifference and embrace risk as well as accountability for others.

When you allow yourself to converge mentally and physically with the experience of another, you generate empathy. Intentionally withholding empathy demands more energy because it forces you to separate yourself from the person you are with. When you keep others out, you also lock yourself in. It is akin to building a defensive moat or a city wall; both can lead to self-incarceration.

When you insulate, you isolate.

When was the last time you felt that the person you were communicating with understood how you were feeling?

When was the last time you shared an experience with a total stranger?

_____

_____

_____

_____

_____

_____

_____

_____

_____

_____

_____

_____

_____

Hypervigilance

Because your emotional expressions always reveal your true feelings or reactions to an experience, it is naïve to believe that others, especially those who have difficulty verbalizing, will not see the contradictions between your words and actions. Individuals who rely on emotional communication—emotional communicators—are finely tuned to the emotional expressions of others. Their ability to predict possible outcomes is much higher than those who rely on spoken words.

Potentially stressful experiences will cause emotional communicators to be hypervigilant with respect to the emotional expressions of others. Hypervigilance can surface when you have a visceral reaction either to seeming deceit in an individual or to the sudden appearance of a stranger whose motives are unclear. Without any conscious effort, you are able to detect signals from their emotional expressions that warn you of potentially dangerous or ulterior motives.

A child can endure a lot of cruelty and indifference just to be accepted, and, for many, belonging outweighs the risk of being harmed. I once faced this predicament from a caregiver's perspective; my challenge was to help a bullied child who did not feel safe enough to point out his abuser. In this instance, I decided not to ask questions; instead, I observed. The tell-tale sign came when the child was in the middle of a board game and other kids were coming in and out of the room. Only the victim was watching the actions of others; he was hypervigilant. Protecting the perpetrator for fear of retaliation is not unusual for victims so I knew his reaction would be either excessive self-control or hidden in its manifestation. When the perpetrator appeared, the victim remained outwardly normal except for the visible pounding of the artery in his neck. This was an indicator of the change in the amount of blood his heart was pumping. Instantly, and as a result of his insecurity, the boy's response system kicked in.

Hypervigilance magnifies and exposes contradictions between words and expressions.

Are you aware of a time you might have made someone else insecure in your presence? What indicators did you notice?

_____

_____

_____

_____

_____

_____

_____

_____

_____

_____

_____

_____

_____

_____

_____

Predetermined Outcomes

When you anticipate an outcome, you essentially predetermine your own response before the event has occurred. Often you assume this mental posture to avoid your own disappointment, loss of control, failure, or rejection. However, this practice locks you into a certain frame of mind that, in turn, prevents you from being receptive to possible changes in others. Predetermining outcomes also makes you vulnerable to the misinterpretation of critical expressions. Consider, for example, the act of holding your arms close to your body. This posture is ambiguous; it could mean that you are cold, afraid, have internal physical pain, or are just plain tired. Rushing to judgment without understanding the *context* in which a person is acting will lead to misjudgment and miscommunication.

Because no two individuals are the same, no two experiences are the same. Pay attention to the details of the person's immediate experience rather than what he or she did in the past or is likely to do in the future. Focus on the here and now and navigate others' expressions with fluid sensitivity. In other words, do not get stuck in your own expectations and calculations. Free yourself from safeguarding your own feelings if you want to ascertain the meaning of emotional expressions. By releasing yourself, you allow emotional expressions to reveal themselves, benefitting all participants in an interaction.

Prejudgment eliminates possibilities.

Recall a time when your predetermined outcomes were inaccu-rate. How did this misjudgment affect you?

_____

_____

_____

_____

_____

_____

_____

_____

_____

_____

_____

_____

_____

_____

_____

Distractions

Personal distractions are like quicksand; they sink your ability to observe. They take away your capacity to respond quickly and leave you with a less accurate observational reading. When distracted, you will miss the subtle movements that express a person's innermost feelings. Most importantly, when you communicate your distraction through your expressions, you insult the person with whom you are communicating. During communication, you must maintain a single objective; multi-tasking and observing emotional expressions are incompatible.

Distractions will always be there; how you choose to manage or minimize them will determine the success of your communication.

Inventory of Your Distractions

1. _____
   _____
   _____

2. _____
   _____
   _____

3. _____
   _____
   _____

4. _____
   _____
   _____

5. _____
   _____
   _____

Goal Fixation

If distractions prevent you from focusing, then goal fixation creates the opposite problem. Goal fixation causes your focus to narrow too much, ultimately weakening your capacity to analyze a situation accurately. Goal fixation prevents you, the observer, from being receptive to the essential details of an experience and its expressions.

When you become fixated on a goal, the fixation determines the approach, which in turn determines the behavior. When this happens, you lose awareness, and you communicate without engaging all of your senses. As you either misread or overlook critical signs of personal security or insecurity, you lose your audience and your communication fails. To succeed, you need to use all of your senses; because fixations prevent you from doing that, they should be avoided. Emotional expressions come before spoken communication, so if you fail at reading emotional cues, then you will fail altogether.

Fixation hides the bend in the road.

In what ways do your own goal fixations hinder or modify your communication with others?

Personal Trappings

True emotional expressions cannot be hidden by clothing, tattoos, or hairstyles. However, material items, such as electronic devices and sunglasses, can serve as smoke screens by attempting to hide insecurities and prop up self-delusion. These are modern shields that deceive you into believing that you are safe, that your personal vulnerabilities are not exposed. Not surprisingly, the social acceptance they provide is tenuous and temporary. A person's internal emotional state will always be uncovered by body movement or lack thereof. Observe closely and emotional expressions of security and insecurity will surface.

The emperor really is naked.

Inventory of Your Trappings

1. _____

_____

_____

2. _____

_____

_____

3. _____

_____

_____

4. _____

_____

_____

5. _____

_____

_____

Importance of our Senses

Humankind seems generally unaware or dismissive of emotional expressions as an essential vehicle for effective communication. Our natural instinct to use all of our senses has been suppressed by cultural conditioning. We were born to use our magnificent sensory capabilities, not to store them away in little boxes of fear and obsession.

In addition to the psychological distractions that alienate us from a sensory experience, we now face technological distractions as well. The use of technology during an interaction limits and isolates the different abilities of our senses. Whenever we confine our senses, we hold ourselves back from full engagement, from bringing our full self to the experience.

We need to rediscover our childhood selves. Young children are masters of Emotional Language because they use and fuse all of their senses. Their reliance on senses more than intellectual ideas or technology allows them to fully discover and engage with the world around them, a practice that we need to recover.

Note: I am not suggesting that a visually- or hearing-impaired individual will be less engaged or less whole. Because differently-abled people rely heavily on the senses that they do have, they may be better emotional communicators than those of us who take our senses for granted. Take full advantage of whatever sensory capabilities you have.

We underestimate the value of that
which is the most innate.

Are you free and able to fully engage your senses? Does the culture of your environment inhibit you?

_____

_____

_____

_____

_____

_____

_____

_____

_____

_____

_____

_____

_____

_____

_____

Vision

When there is too much to see or you do not know how to manage the information, you begin to learn how not to see. Being able to distinguish the details within your field of vision seems, on appearance, like an easy task. However, you need to make a conscious effort to remain engaged during an interaction; otherwise, you may sink into your own thoughts and merely give an appearance of "looking." This self-absorption can happen when you anticipate another person's thoughts or actions and begin to formulate your own at the same time. Learning to "see" requires a high degree of self-control over your thoughts and distractions; otherwise they blur your vision. You cannot invest in another's well-being while thinking of your own; making them your visual and mental priority is essential for seeing the finer details of their emotional expressions.

What causes you to lose visual and mental focus of the person you are with?

Hearing

Sound informs us of what has just happened or is about to happen. Have you ever noticed how acutely animals detect and respond to the slightest sounds in their environment? Dogs are particularly adept at discerning whether the sound of footsteps is of a family member returning or a stranger approaching. This skill is not a monopoly of dogs; you, too, may cultivate and apply it in your daily interactions.

Listen for the various properties of sound—tone, pitch, vibration—and be aware of their duration and frequency. These can alert you to the impact that an experience is having on you or the speaker. Notice the pauses or the absences of sound as well as the sounds made by other body parts. When a person walks, for instance, the noise of the footsteps can tell you how much weight he places on his feet, providing an abundance of information about his physical and /or mental state.

This level of hearing must be cultivated. First, minimize the extraneous sounds from artificial sources that bombard you daily, such as radios, cell phones, and televisions. To connect and extrapolate information from the sounds humans make, you need intimate exposure to the source of that sound—the person.

What properties of sound do you tend to detect in others that may indicate a change in their mental or physical state?

_____

_____

_____

_____

_____

_____

_____

_____

_____

_____

_____

_____

_____

_____

_____

_____

Smell

Before maps, road signs, and global positioning systems existed, humans relied on their keen sense of smell to recognize, assess, and interact with their environment. It is something we still do when we identify our mothers before we can open our eyes, follow the smell of freshly baked bread, and recognize it is time to change the cat litter.

Because scent has no shape, color, physical weight or texture, it is easily undervalued or forgotten. However, scent directs you to each other's physiological and psychological focus, need, and condition as well as to your environmental surroundings. This orientation provides security and comfort, which, in turn, offers confidence.

Your ability to access information through smell is determined by your familiarity with the odor, how receptive you are to smell, and how appropriately you contextualize it. Proximity and context (Is the odor reflective of the environment? Does it corroborate with the verbal information?) are the two main ingredients to keep in mind when determining the value or even the presence of a scent and its possible effects. To register an odor, the human nose needs to be very close to the source of the smell. Even then, your ability to smell consciously is limited. Keep in mind that unless there is a contrasting odor present or a sudden absence of the odor is noticed, you will quickly acclimate to it and lose the opportunity to learn its value.

Are you able to recognize anyone by his or her odor? If so, how close do you need to be?

_____

_____

_____

_____

_____

_____

_____

_____

_____

_____

_____

_____

_____

Touch

We are tactile beings. Touching is central in a trusting relationship; being able to touch or be touched alters the dynamics in a relationship. It is equally capable of empowering and disempowering. A simple touch carries with it the possibility of great affection and tenderness or of gross violation of trust and power. Because touch is an intimate act, it cannot be taken lightly, especially in the context of emotional communication. It is touch that will ultimately cement the bond of trust and acceptance.

The space that exists between two people will define and expose the quality of their relationship, as will the tenderness or rigidity of their contact. It is the absence of power or force behind a touch that extends trust and kindness. Martial artists train to access relevant information through touch in order to counteract a physical attack; yet, mothers know the value and meaning of touch instinctively.

Think back to an experience of being in physical contact and how that made you feel. What about that touch created feelings of security and comfort or insecurity and discomfort?

Sensitivity of our Senses

If you have ever launched a paper boat in a stream or puddle, you know how sensitive it is to the slightest ripple or breeze. It dances on the surface of the water as it tries to stay afloat. If it is too heavy or porous, it will soak up the water and sink. If it is too light, it will capsize. The boat is sensitive to how it is made and to all the elements that surround it. Connecting to and cultivating your vision, hearing, touch, and smell requires the sensitivity of a paper boat. Once you acquire it, you can access an ocean of information. Sensitivity connects you intimately to the changing emotional conditions within you and the person with whom you are communicating. It also allows you to understand the conditions that surround and influence you both.

I recognize that for some the words "sensitivity" and "emotional" denote weakness or a lack of strength, but these are not flaws or vulnerabilities. Connecting with your emotions, as well as those of others', empowers you; it provides necessary stamina to respond to the changing needs of a person. Without sensitivity in communication, the conversation becomes a one-sided engagement devoid of consideration.

I recall a lesson I learned in a gym that I frequented as a young adult. Everyone there was cordial, and acknowledging each other's presence was the accepted norm. However, there was one man who never acknowledged me regardless of how many ways I attempted to greet him. I quickly concluded that he must be racist. I held that judgment until one day, to my horror, I overheard him speaking to another member, and I realized immediately that he was hearing impaired. When I had previously greeted him, he quite literally had not heard me. The embarrassment I felt from this discovery made me crumble; I was weighed down by this realization, for it was I who was impaired. How easy it is to become ignorant in the presence of those who cannot conventionally hear our demands? You and I become disabled when we are unaware of each other's condition or needs.

Sensitivity allows you to be aware of
and receptive to all possibilities.

Do you have a story of your own sensitivity or insensitivity?

Daily Practice of
Self-Control, Self-Awareness, and Presence of Mind

Integrating Emotional Language into your daily communication requires your active participation. This engagement, in turn, requires the daily practice of self-control, self-awareness, and presence of mind. *Self-control* prevents impulsive actions or reactions; *self-awareness* makes you conscious of your impact on others; *presence of mind* gives you the ability to involve all your senses.

Below, I list some approaches you can employ in your daily interactions. After assessing your current habits, set goals for using these approaches more effectively or more frequently. Your progress toward achieving true communication and understanding will be determined by the quality of—and your commitment to—daily practice.

This self-evaluation will provide insight into how you engage with and may be experienced by others.

Place an "X" along the scale to indicate the approach you use when engaging with others.

Involvement: *I engage in the experience to provide support and promote unity.*

| Consistently | Selectively | Not at all |

Example and/or thoughts:

_____

_____

_____

_____

Empathy: *I feel from the other's perspective.*

| Consistently | Selectively | Not at all |

Example and/or thoughts:

_____

_____

_____

_____

Trust: *I keep all of my commitments.*

Consistently   *Selectively*   *Not at all*

Example and/or thoughts:

Patience: *I allow experiences to progress naturally.*

Consistently   *Selectively*   *Not at all*

Example and/or thoughts:

Humility: *I consider all tasks and contributions to be significant.*

Consistently   *Selectively*   *Not at all*

Example and/or thoughts:

Humor: *I use humor regularly.*

_____

Consistently   Selectively   Not at all

Example and/or thoughts:

_____

_____

_____

Availability: *I make myself accessible by actively removing barriers.*

_____

Consistently   Selectively   Not at all

Example and/or thoughts:

_____

_____

_____

Fluidity: *I am creative and adaptable.*

_____

Consistently   Selectively   Not at all

Example and/or thoughts:

_____

_____

_____

Helping: *I exceed others' expectations.*

Consistently   *Selectively*   *Not at all*

Example and/or thoughts:

_____

_____

_____

_____

Timing: *I introduce a word, idea, or experience in the appropriate context, at the appropriate time, and with the appropriate speed.*

Consistently   *Selectively*   *Not at all*

Example and/or thoughts:

_____

_____

_____

_____

CHAPTER THREE

EMOTIONAL EXPRESSIONS

The following section offers an explanation of what insecurity and security mean in the context of your ability to communicate and interact effectively. This continuum is broad, long, and deep; it is limited only by your lack of experience or the perception of what might happen. Consider the question: Within this immediate experience, am I 1) comfortable or uncomfortable and/or 2) safe or unsafe? This is not a question you consciously ask yourself or pause to reflect on during an experience. However, you answer these questions instinctively, through your emotional expressions.

Not all expressions of insecurity or security are fully visible, but keen observers will make the most of what they do sense. The expressions have a surfacing point, but the amount of time spent on the surface varies. Some are apparent throughout the interaction; others fade away at the very moment of inception. What you are aiming for is refining your ability to detect the inception points of an expression; this can be achieved through the cultivation of your sensory awareness. In addition, all expressions need to be kept within the context of each individual experience.

Influence of Insecurity on Communication

Insecurity in yourself or others determines how effectively you can communicate with and understand others. Insecurity suspends your mental and physical calm and disrupts your normal bodily functions. It can be caused by health-related factors, external threats of physical harm, loss of social acceptance, or the presence of social judgment. The sources of insecurity are as vast and as varied as your imagination.

If you fail to recognize and evaluate emotional expressions caused by insecurities, you cannot communicate effectively. The significance of feeling insecure is relative; if the person who is experiencing it can withstand the anxiety and normalize the situation, then the insecurity may not significantly affect the communication. If the person is unaware of the source of his or her insecurity or cannot control it, then it will undermine the communication.

The degree to which the experience impacts the body will be communicated by the intensity of the emotional expressions. Only when the source of the insecurity is under control will anxiety dissipate, allowing for a relaxed physical state and a positive interaction. A relaxed physical state is indicated through a smile or relaxed facial muscles and the exposure of vulnerable body parts.

The gravity of an experience is relative to one's ability to ensure security.

Vulnerable Body Parts
Head
Neck
Abdomen
Genitals
Limbs when extended

Insecurity
Requires concentrated use of energy to establish control or domi-
nate the source of the experience
Produces mental and physical disorientation, disruption, and break-
down
Creates a sense of loss of control

Sources of Insecurity
Disease or medical condition
Injury
Agitation
Discomfort
Loss of physical and/or mental capacity
Physical threat
Presence or perception of social judgment
Lack of social acceptance
Competitive social group

Result of Insecurity
Concentrated physical function
Contracted muscles
Collapse of bodily function or loss of coordination
Employment of coping behaviors
Receptive only to the information that ensures security
Loss or decline of memory
Dissipation of problem solving skills
Diminished ability to speak clearly

Expressions of Insecurity

Detecting emotional expressions is within everyone's ability; however, it requires the practice of self-control, self-awareness, and presence of mind. Since emotional expressions reflect your immediate experience, you do not have an opportunity to repeat or relive them. Thus, total involvement is required by all participants during communication.

Listed below is a sampling of emotional expressions we all display. Keep in mind some expressions are too intangible or subtle to describe.

Head and Face
> Head is rigid
> Head shakes
> Head suddenly moves up or away
> Head moves from side to side
> Face color changes
> Face is puffy
> Forehead wrinkles
> Brow furrows
> Nostrils flare
> Not smiling
> Hands cover face

Eyes
> Aimless or rapid movement
> Pupils constrict
> Quick glance
> Eyes stare down or away
> Eyes dazed, glazed, or stunned
> Eyes wide open
> Eyelids flutter or close
> Tears

Mouth
> Jaws clench
> Mouth is dry

Biting lips
Lips are dry
Lips licked constantly
Lips twitching
Tongue protrudes
Holding the breath
Breathing is shallow, rapid, or erratic
Difficulty or excessive swallowing

Voice

Crackles
Volume rises or disappears
Pitch unusually high or low
Speech rhythm is erratic
Speaking out of the corner of the mouth
Speaking under the breath

Neck and Shoulders

Neck stiffens
Neck swells
Pulse visible in neck
Touch or rub neck
Shoulders rigid
Shoulders are raised to make the neck disappear
Shoulders hang down
Shoulder shrugs
Back turned

Arms and Hands

Arms crossed and hands clasped
Arm movements restricted, kept closer to the body, or hidden
Arms dangling or limp
Arms suddenly move upwards
Arms and hands flail
Hand movements restricted, kept closer to the body, or hidden
Hands hold objects tightly
Hands sweaty

Fists clenched
Sucking thumb
Bite nails or cuticles

Chest and Abdomen

Chest expands or contracts
Chest and abdomen move back and away
Chest or abdomen covered with arms or objects
Abdomen contracts

Buttocks, Legs, and Feet

Hips and buttocks misalign with the direction of feet
Rubbing thigh or calf
Legs and feet bounce or wiggle
Leg muscles tighten
Legs cross or knees press together
Legs or feet wrap around chairs, table legs, or other objects
Legs and feet point away from the direction of the conversation or interaction
Feet crossed
Feet firmly planted on the ground

Other Expressions of Insecurity

Vulnerable body parts protected
Low or high tolerance for sensory perception
Body positioned for response
Body expanded or puffed
Control or anchor physical movements
Misaligned or out of balance body movements
Shaking or trembling
Easily startled
Change in body temperature
Loss of facial and body symmetry

Blending in a group
Physically attaching to familiar people, animals, or objects
Minimizing movement by sitting or lying down

Making wide turns while walking
Obstruct pathways of others
Lean away from the shared space of interaction
Exclusion from self-determined/desired social group
Urgency to finish the task at hand
Avoid or ignore the task at hand
Not cooperate by moving slowly or erratically, postponing, or cancelling

Move, rearrange, hold onto, or block with objects
Repetitive touching of clothing or personal trappings
Self-grooming
Self-mutilation
Excessive eating or drinking
Frequent urination
Constipation or defecation
Sleepy
Disorientation

Inventory of Your Expressions of Insecurity

1. _____

_____

_____

2. _____

_____

_____

3. _____

_____

_____

4. _____

_____

_____

5. _____

_____

_____

Response Systems

When you confine your understanding and application of a subject to its existing definition, you deprive yourself of knowing how it evolves, how else it can be applied, and the nuances it possesses. Understanding human behavior and, in particular, communication requires you to pursue the in-betweens, the subtleties and intangibles. Here, within the generally understood response systems such as "fight-or-flight", I have included some of the in-betweens. You may discover that you have some of your own.

How you cope with insecurities can be best observed through the following responses: when you flee, hide, mask, soothe, freeze, fight, surrender, or accept defeat. Observing them during an interaction and evaluating the probability of possible behavior will facilitate a more fluid interaction. Each coping mechanism can be viewed along a continuum, depending on its intensity and visibility (whether it is overt or concealed).

Flight

Avoid the source of insecurity by running, walking or moving away.

Hide

Conceal or barricade whole or part of the body; avoid eye contact; deny or fabricate scenarios; become anonymous or blend in.

Mask

Project an aggressive or nonchalant appearance; appear busy; force or fake a smile, comedic animation, or self ridicule; use excessive or exaggerated behavior.

Soothe

Self-pacify or massage different parts of the body; be engrossed in another activity; smoke, drink, eat, hum, sing, or use gadgets.

Freeze

Become motionless, either partially or completely; hold limbs close to the body to reduce physical size and body movement; become silent.

Fight

Risk harm to self and others to gain control of the situation and create a pathway to escape.

Surrender

Temporary withdrawal due to physical or mental exhaustion or incapacitation; however, resurgence or escape remain possible.

Defeat

Allow others to manipulate or control the body and mind because all other coping mechanisms (both physical and mental) have been exhausted or cannot be considered as options.

Influence of Security on Communication

When you are secure, you become relaxed and have all of your senses at your disposal. A relaxed mind and body do not waste energy fending off insecurities. They fuse, optimizing your awareness of—and connection with—people on multiple dimensions. When you are secure, you can help others relax, which in turn makes you even more relaxed. When a connection is made in a relaxed state, the resulting communication will refresh you, giving you even more energy with which to manage new experiences. However, engagement in unwarranted actions during a conversation, such as taking a call, texting, gazing elsewhere, or power posturing, can make others insecure, requiring you to reengage in the conversation to move it forward. This process of disengagement and reengagement wastes time.

Loss of security can also occur more subtly. The elements of social judgment and acceptance can greatly influence your ability to communicate effectively. For instance, when you realize a subject being discussed is beyond your current ability to comprehend, you may remain silent for fear of social judgment. Similarly, the harder you try to be socially accepted, the more difficult it may become for you to communicate your ideas and experiences. Because security is so fragile, you should embrace all opportunities to not only make yourself more secure but also to protect the security of others.

Security casts a light over the unknown.

Vulnerable Body Parts
Head
Neck
Abdomen
Genitals
Limbs when extended

Security
Optimize use of energy for normal mental and physical functions
Produce mental and physical clarity, power, control, opportunity, and creativity

Sources
Free of disease or medical condition
Free of injury or chronic pain
Free of agitation
Comfort
Physical and mental capacity to manage new experiences
Absence of threat or loss of control
Social acceptance
Positive support from family and friends
Non-competitive social group

Result
Supple and relaxed muscles
Normal physical and mental functions
Cooperative and pro-social behavior
Receptivity to information from multiple sources
Enhanced memory
Strengthened problem solving skills
Desire to communicate verbally

Expressions of Security

Making eye contact
Exposing vulnerable body parts
Permitting touch
Leaning into shared space
Creating a pathway to give and receive body contact
Cooperating socially

Moving closer to others
Relaxing muscles
Participation
Displaying optimism
Contributing willingly
Taking risks

Inventory of Your Expressions of Security

1. _____

_____

_____

2. _____

_____

_____

3. _____

_____

_____

4. _____

_____

_____

5. _____

_____

_____

Helping Others to Relax and Feel Secure

Recognize or acknowledge the individual
Establish a ritual for greeting and departing
Engage in a conversation that focuses on kindness and generosity
Have a collective approach and use "we" as opposed to "you" or "me"
Touch appropriately
Avoid staring

Offer social acceptance
Offer refreshment or food
Offer seating
Offer comfort
Offer a neutral environment when possible
Offer an exit route; avoid creating a sense of either physical or mental
entrapment

Project a relaxed demeanor both in behavior and language
Be patient
Connect the expected experience to a prior positive experience
Empower by receiving whatever the individual can offer by way of
time, ideas, or physical effort as a mark of commitment and trust
Cultivate trust by taking risks yourself

Do not push the individual to verbalize feelings
Avoid preferential treatment towards others
Avoid creating a rushed atmosphere
Put away personal distractions: food, books, magazines, electronics
Seek permission if your attention needs to be diverted
Remove sunglasses
Avoid wearing clothing that represents power or authority

What do you do to help others relax and feel secure?

Experiential Impact and Memory

Experiential impact is the result of intersecting with an experience—the way it alters and reshapes your world view, how it manifests in your body and mind, and how you cope with the present and prepare for the future. Discussing an experience, you might uncover many details and even find the value of the experience, but sensory perception defines its true experiential impact in how it resides in your memory over time. When an experience is integrated at a sensory level, we retain it more dynamically.

I have learned not to measure the impact of an experience by the details of each goal achieved or other quantifiable outcomes. Instead, I focus on whether the experience was oppressive or liberating, painful or joyful, suffocating or life-giving, disempowering or empowering, confining or freeing.

I learned the nature and value of experiential impact and its influence on memory from a female client with severe memory loss that required physical activity. Week to week, I arrived to help her, but she could not remember the details of any experience, including my name. While I was on vacation, I arranged for a colleague to cover her sessions for me. Upon returning, I learned that she refused to work with anyone else. It was the nature of our initial experience that influenced her loyalty to me. Even though she could not remember the details from our previous experiences, she had an innate awareness of her extreme personal vulnerability, a vulnerability that demanded predictability and a reliance on others for security.

We all have the ability to recognize an experience, or strands of it, consciously or unconsciously. The weight, meaning, and color of a memory are influenced by the emotional security or insecurity resulting from the experience. If you base an experience purely on its details, you will underestimate an individual's ability to remember and react to your presence. Ultimately, the feeling of an experience is left indelibly in all of us.

When you intersect with an experience and gather the information with your senses, the impact is not lost; it is left in you. A tiny pebble dropped in a large pool of water may disappear from sight, yet it still remains, occupying a space and creating a presence. However, you realize its physical existence only when you step on it. Like a pebble, your memory has its own presence and meaning in your life as it tumbles across the landscape of your mind, and its importance is realized only when you are reminded of it.

It is the experience of security or insecurity that defines our relationship with each other.

CHAPTER FOUR

STANDARDS OF PRACTICE

Standards of practice are essential for an equitable process of communication. To counteract our innate desire to exploit personal positions of advantage, we need to engage and disengage from encounters carefully with empathy to protect those who are vulnerable.

Rules of Engagement

Rules of engagement govern how you engage initially and how you manage disengagement. Entry and exit points define how well you have communicated during the interaction. These points indicate transitions as you move from one experience to another. This is not unlike astronauts entering and exiting the earth's atmosphere. The speed and point of entry will determine the safety and the quality of the passenger's flight. Communication between people is the convergence of both the physical and mental atmospheres each person represents.

In an initial communication experience, be aware of and use Emotional Language so that you can adjust your behavior and language during the conversation. If you ignore Emotional Language, the interaction will, more than likely, be haphazard and fraught with misunderstanding or even hostility. When insecurity precedes an encounter, it is subsequently either reinforced or replaced by security during the encounter; when insecurity is reinforced, productive communication is compromised. Therefore, establishing security is paramount; it supersedes all other needs and wants. A sense of control over the interaction must be extended to others who seek to attain security.

To establish a sense of security when parting, disengagement requires as much sensitivity and awareness as does engagement. The other individual needs to feel a sense of control over the disengagement process. Ending an engagement creates insecurity or uncertainty because leaving brings to an end, for the time being, the support, bond, and understanding provided during the interaction. When disengagement goes well, the person will look forward to reengagement.

The impending transition to the next interaction also influences the disengagement process. Here, if support is necessary, it needs to be acknowledged and provided; doing so brings security, which makes the person mentally and physically willing to disengage.

The delicate nature of this process of connecting and disconnecting was reinforced to me by a nonverbal client who was very shy and anxious about such transitions. To greet him, I learned to wait with one hand open, palm facing up and slightly extended every time we met. When the time was right, he would touch the palm of my hand with either his finger or his whole hand, depending on his internal level of need. I learned that shaking, holding, or clasping hands was not an option. Even though it was a very slight and momentary exchange of physical contact, it let me know how he was feeling and was a symbolic gesture of his trust in me. Allowing him to establish the terms of our contact provided him with control and increased security.

The disengagement process was also within his control. It started the moment the desire to end a particular activity or return home was expressed. On one occasion, the moment of uncertainty for him came in the form of a sudden downpour. The heavy rain completely obscured our ability to see the direction in which we were driving. I was alerted to what it meant to him by the way he suddenly leaned forward and touched the windshield with a long exhalation and a vocal tone of concern as if to try and remove the blinding blanket of rain. His insecurity was addressed after I found a safe place to stop while we waited for the storm to pass. I explained that we were still heading to his home and requested his permission to take another road where we could drive safely.

Along with my explanation, I drew a map of the detour explaining where we were, the normal route, and the new road we would be taking. I have found that attaching visual information, more often than not, solidifies, reinforces, and holds firmly in place the accompanying verbal information. Making multiple sensory connections to information reduces misinterpretation and reinforces understanding. He arrived at his destination with a high level of control and sense of achievement in having coped with the sudden change in our plans. This experience gave me an opportunity to earn his trust for the next experiential detour.

Empathy is the prerequisite for effective engagement and disengagement.

What rules of engagement do you employ?
Do you tailor your engagement to individual needs?
Do you request permission from others to engage or disengage?

_____

_____

_____

_____

_____

_____

_____

_____

_____

_____

_____

_____

_____

_____

_____

Power in Communication

The word power, both physical and intellectual, evokes many associations, meanings, and implications. For some, power conjures up the idea of domination and exploitation; for others, it represents the ability to defend and preserve an idea, territory, or the self. In all cases, it provides the person in the position of power the opportunity to have an effect on others. Who speaks and who listens indicates where the power lies in a relationship. What is said also matters. In a statement like, "You need to understand what I am saying," the speaker determines what is important and whose thoughts and feelings have priority. The speaker's claim reinforces his or her position of power. Both speakers and listeners want to be understood; being understood is an innate psychological need that not only establishes and enhances a sense of belonging but also preserves self-determination.

The resistance that culminated in the war I experienced as a child was based on the right to be heard and to speak the native language. This unique national struggle for the liberation and independence of an entire country was rooted in a language movement. The equity of power that is lost is the same between two as it is between two million. The freedom to be heard is a fundamental human right, whether it is stated or not. Individuals who communicate verbally have immense power over those who cannot. Whether an inability to articulate verbally lasts a moment or a lifetime, the outcome is the same—inequity.

Without the ability to communicate and to be understood, people become socially isolated and lose their sense of self-worth. To better illustrate this point, imagine yourself to be a person who either cannot speak the dominant language or is not articulate enough to state your personal needs (to ensure a sense of security). How would you feel? What would you do?

If you possess mental and physical ability, then you have power in communication. Therefore, you have a responsibility to temper or rein it in; otherwise, it can become a destructive and oppressive force. Think about those who are vulnerable, those whose quality of experience you determine at any given moment. Abuses of power occur often between parents and children, teachers and students, and social workers and clients, but you have power over anyone to whom you extend your support, so the possibilities for inequitable, damaging communication are vast.

How do you empower those who are unable to verbally express their securities and insecurities?

Ethics in Using Emotional Language

Using your knowledge of another person's emotional expressions responsibly requires great tact and consideration. You must be mindful not to take advantage of or manipulate an individual's predicament and behavior. Using Emotional Language, you can understand someone who is unable to verbally articulate his or her needs. Therefore, you have an ethical duty to practice empathy and use the least amount of personal power or force needed to ensure the safety and well-being of another. When this ethical standard is set aside or modified, equity is compromised and communication is undermined.

Professed ethics without empathy is hollow morality.

How is an individual compromised when ethical standards are not preserved?

emotional language

CHAPTER FIVE

THE INFLUENCE OF SCIENCE

In this chapter, I discuss the significance of two systems that are essential in understanding the biological framework of Emotional Language. Their presence is undeniable; their function is indisputable; and their impact on how we experience and perceive the world around us is incalculable. By understanding how these systems work, their components and mechanics, we gain a more concrete and clear picture of a language that is intimate, yet universal.

The Biology of an Experience

Emotions are the result of a biological process that takes place within your body. The ability to sense, evaluate, decide, and react to an experience is at the heart of Emotional Language. The body is a universe unto its own. Therefore, it behooves you to peer inside and better understand how emotions are expressed. In so doing, you learn how to explore the implications of an experience.

I present the subject of Emotional Language from a multi-dimensional perspective in an effort to provide a comprehensive explanation. The body has many complex operating systems; these comprise groups of structures and their functions. I have selected both the nervous system and the muscular system to demonstrate the mechanical processes that take place when we are affected by an experience. Experiences manifest themselves in other systems as well; they are not confined solely to these areas.

Sensory nerves are the ones that inform your brain of what is going on inside and outside of your body. They keep you connected to your internal and external worlds. It is critical to learn about the nervous system first because the brain is at the core of this system, and it ultimately defines the meaning of your experiences.

The Nervous System

The nervous system can be seen as the detector, messenger, decision maker, and executor of the body. It has two operating systems: 1) the brain and central nervous system and 2) the peripheral nervous system. Let me first define the terms *nerve* and *system*.

First, the nerve is a conducting or message-carrying tissue. Two types of nerve fibers, the sensory and the motor nerve fiber, spread throughout the body. Second, a set of task- specific nerves make up a system. Just as the wiring of a house allows for the operation of different household appliances, so too does the body's nervous system facilitate the exchange of information to keep you functioning as one unit running different parts of the body. Each system relies on the other to fulfill its purpose. Even the brain is useless without other systems, particularly the special sensors.

Let's take this systems approach one step further and imagine that each one of us individually represents a sensory system that probes and experiences life uniquely. As you connect with others, you become more aware of your environment, so your awareness increases in proportion with the number and variety of your connections. When you emotionally and empathetically touch another person or any other life form, you metaphorically create the invisible nerve tissue that transports the impulse to your greater self or greater intelligence; this process enables you to understand and appreciate the world around you. This fusion of reliance, the interdependence of humans and all other living systems, completes the circle of life; it allows living creatures to fulfill their true potential.

As the name suggests, the sensory nerve endings are the ones that sense and gather information such as smell or pain and take it to the brain. The motor nerves receive their instructions from the brain and activate the movements in your body. For example, the facial motor nerves control the muscles for your facial expressions.

Different nerves create different nerve impulses, or energy, to communicate with the brain. Nerves have different purposes and are present throughout your entire body. You have the optic nerve for sight, the auditory nerve for sound, the vestibular nerve for balance, the trigeminal nerve for touch, the olfactory nerve for smell, and the glossopharyngeal nerve for taste. The brain, the seat of intelligence, is responsible for the interpretation of all information. It is an organ made of nervous tissue with three regions: hind, mid, and fore brain. Each has its own subdivisions of responsibility for different functions. Since the capacity to use your brain represents intelligence, your capacity to emotionally evaluate and respond also represents intelligence. The limbic system, or the heart of your brain, makes the emotional evaluation of an experience possible. It is not isolated or compartmentalized within the brain; it is part of--and interconnected with--the rest of the brain and located deep inside.

The brain is at the core of the *central nervous system*, the chief processor and evaluator of information as well as the initiator of messages to different parts of the body for appropriate actions. When a sensory nerve ending detects an internal or external stimulus or change, it creates a nerve impulse that then travels via the nerve fibers and up the spinal cord to the brain. All messages are delivered via the spinal cord, a column of nerve fibers that are part of the central nervous system and that run down the inside of the backbone from the brain to the lower back. The spinal cord, the information highway, is connected to the *peripheral nervous system*. The peripheral nervous system, which is connected to the organs and the muscles, relays messages between the central nervous system, the sense organs, and the muscles.

During an experience of insecurity, the *autonomic nervous system* regulates the organs and blood flow based on the experiential need of the body. This system has two components: the *sympathetic* and *parasympathetic* nervous systems, each with distinct capabilities. An experience of insecurity will trigger the sympathetic nervous system into action, and an appropriate physical action will follow. It may trigger the heart to beat faster to redirect the blood to the muscles, so they can react quickly. After the crisis has passed, the parasympathetic nervous system will trigger the slowing down of the heart, normalizing the blood flow, and restarting normal bodily functions. A helpful description for remembering these distinctions is that the sympathetic system helps us with "fight or flight" responses, while the parasympathetic system prepares us for "rest and digest."

Special Sensors

Emotional Language is possible because of the cumulative effect of sensory capabilities and awareness. We all possess five special sensors-- sight, sound, touch, taste, and smell-- that stimulate specific regions of the brain. Your ability to communicate and interact depends on your sensory sensitivity and capacity. Disorientation and confusion occur when they are not functioning optimally. If left unchecked and uncared for, sensors can deteriorate and become inefficient.

Vision

The eye and the brain allow us to see; however, light makes vision possible. Light bouncing off objects in all directions is captured by the eye and interpreted by the brain. It travels in a straight line through two lenses, the cornea and the iris. Together they control the light and focus the image, making it ready for the retina. In the retina, sensors or photoreceptors convert the light into impulses that travel along the optic nerve to the brain. Whether your brain sees black and white or color is determined by two different receptors. Rods and cones are the photoreceptors (light receptors) of the retina. Rods determine black and white while cones determine color.

Hearing

What you hear are actually vibrations in the air known as sound waves. The pitch of the sound is determined by the frequency of vibrations, and the size of the vibrations determines the perceived volume.

The ear is divided into three parts—outer, middle, and inner. The outer ear or the pinna captures the sound, which then travels through the ear canal to the eardrum in the middle ear, where the mechanics of bones amplify the vibrations. The vibrations travel to the inner ear, where the cochlear nerve converts them into impulses that travel to the brain.

Another overlooked, but highly critical, function of the ear is that it provides your sense of balance. This state of equilibrium results from your ear's constant monitoring of the position of your head. Like a carpenter's level that is used to hang a picture, the inner ear has fluid-filled tubes that detect changes in the head's position. The vestibular nerve transmits impulses to the brain, communicating that the body should realign itself to achieve balance.

Touch

Your skin is the protective covering for your body and the interface that receives mechanical and thermal energy from the outside world. The different concentration levels of sensory nerves under the skin determine the sensitivity of different parts of your body. Hairless parts of the body such as lips have greater numbers of sensory receptors. However, at the base of your hair are also touch receptors that respond to the lightest contact.

The skin senses temperature, pain, contact, and pressure. The skin's nerves send impulses to the brain, which then interprets the value of the touch. The type of contact determines the speed in which the brain receives this message.

Taste and Smell

Only primary tastes (sweet and sour, bitter and salty) are sensed by the tongue. The tongue is covered by mucous membranes (thin tissue that excretes a slippery moist secretion made of salt, water, and proteins) and the papillae (the rough surface of the tongue).

All other tastes are evaluated by smell. You become aware of an odor when the receptor nerves in the nasal cavity's mucous membrane convey a message to the brain. Your awareness of the odor dissipates rapidly because your nose secretes lots of mucous, so smells must be identified and evaluated quickly.

The Muscular System

Without muscles there is no movement. You need muscles to sense, to communicate, and to observe expressions. Muscles allow you to act; they are flexible and elastic engines of your body that take you places and let you do things you both like and dislike.

There are three types of muscle tissues—skeletal, smooth, and cardiac. The *skeletal muscles* give your body the shape it has. They are under your voluntary control, and they are attached to your bones by tendons; however, the facial muscles that dictate your facial expressions are directly attached to your skin. The major skeletal muscles move your limbs in deliberate opposition. When one muscle in a pair contracts or pulls, the other relaxes or extends. Arm muscles, such as biceps and triceps, work in this way. They move when the brain triggers instructional impulses that are carried by the motor nerves. These muscles are in a constant state of partial contraction caused by nerve impulses. They produce muscle *tone* and maintain a constant state of immediate action readiness.

In contrast, the *smooth muscles* are less obvious; they regulate the size of the pupil of your eyes and are also found in your organ walls. The smooth muscle that works nonstop and keeps you alive is the *cardiac muscle*; it regulates the blood flow for your entire body. There are two types of smooth muscle fibers. Slow twitch fibers maintain posture and provide muscle strength and endurance; fast twitch fibers regulate rapid or sudden movements, such as eye or facial movements.

It will be difficult to fully appreciate the role muscles play during communication if you cannot first recognize them in yourself. Notice the process of contraction and relaxation of your muscles that causes movement. When you move, investigate that movement with your fingers; keeping your hand open, touch the skin where movement is occurring and become familiar with its operation. Notice the intensity and the speed of the muscle contraction; these factors determine the amount of energy necessary for the movement.

CHAPTER SIX

MASTERING
EMOTIONAL LANGUAGE

This chapter features case studies that demonstrate the effectiveness of Emotional Language within vulnerable populations who are either unable or unwilling to verbally articulate their needs. I examine the ways in which I leveraged the critical elements of Emotional Language, their primary method of communication, to effectively interact with them. Finally, I have included sample exercises to help you enhance your sensory awareness and increase your proficiency in Emotional Language.

The Run

Scenario

How does a young adult with autism experience running when exercise has not been part of his normal activity? Consider, in addition, this individual's typical apprehension and resistance to any new activity.

Applying Emotional Language

As I walked with this client, I encouraged and reassured him through physical contact. On this particular occasion, we walked with our arms gently pressing against each other.

This mild contact provided me with instant feedback on the slightest muscle contraction or physical change in his body in response to what he was experiencing. This physical proximity allowed me to preserve a visual awareness of movement, using my peripheral vision, without having to turn my head and look directly at the client.

As I felt changes in his arm as well as looked and listened for any change in the visual and audible landscape, I also maintained an awareness of the ground below, of what I felt under my feet. This was critical information because this particular client walked with his instep facing forward, making it easy for him to trip if the ground was uneven or unpredictable. As people on the path passed in both directions, I detected nothing unusual until I heard someone running towards us from behind. I remained alert and sensitive to the moment our path intersected with the runner. As the runner jogged past us, my client did not lean into our shared space; instead, he leaned out of our shared space the moment he saw the runner. His upper body projected forward in an effort to emulate the running motion. His momentary mirroring was my opportunity. Without hesitation, we started to run.

Critical Elements:

Observation
>Stayed attuned to my client and the environment

Tracking
>Monitored the changes in the environment and within my client
>Heard the footsteps of the runner
>Felt the contraction of my client's muscles, emulating the runner
>Saw the forward projection of my client's body into the runner's space

Sensitivity
>Maintained a fluid sensitivity to my client and the environment
>Became aware the moment my client desired to imitate the runner

Critical Response Time
>Responded quickly to the changes in the environment and my client
>Used mental and physical energy to respond without resistance or hesitation

Distance and Empathy
>Aligned with my client's physical and emotional vulnerability and coordinated our rhythm of movement

Predetermined Outcome
>Avoided calculating the impact of the passing runner

Distractions
>Uncertainty of the passing runner's affect on my client was transformed from a distraction into an opportunity

Goal Fixation
>Did not take him running; rather, facilitated the running when he desired it

The Assignment

Scenario
How can the involvement and dignity of a senior citizen be preserved in a challenging group activity?

Applying Emotional Language
While participating in a craft activity with a group of seniors at a day care facility, I was sitting at a table next to an individual who was very jovial. Our task was to cut out pre-drawn patterns from a large but slippery piece of cloth. While others at the table eagerly started cutting with their scissors, I noticed a very slight retraction or sinking of the person's body mass further into her chair. This was followed by a delay in expressing any desire to pick up the scissors and get started. I encouraged her involvement by offering my assistance. She agreed to work collectively, although her physical expressions demonstrated her reluctance. Her hand moved forward towards the scissors, yet her fingers remained pointing towards her body with a closed fist.

It was then that I realized her internal desire to have her arm and hand close to her body. She was reluctant to participate because she feared inadequacy in executing the task. She did not want to expose her weakness. So, I shifted her focus from picking up the scissors to the difficulty of handling the material by one person. I suggested we needed two people to accomplish this task, one to hold and one to cut. This made her sit up and lean into our shared space, expressing her desire to continue. I gave her the option to hold or to cut. She chose to hold. We were able to complete the project collectively and cheerfully.

Through my observation and awareness of her environment and expressions, I was able to guide her through a challenging experience while preserving her dignity. Exposure to social judgment was the least tangible of all the elements, yet it yielded a great influence (at first negative and then positive) on her desire to participate in the activity.

Critical Elements:

Observation
Recognized the limitation of physical movement
Recognized the challenge presented by the scissors and materials

Tracking
Monitored the progression of each expression:
1) Initially cheerful, 2) Retraction into the chair, 3) Tentative efforts 4) Cooperation and sitting up, 5) Participation and effort 6) Completion of task

Sensitivity
Possibility of social judgment: peers judging her ability as adequate or inadequate
Physical ability required to operate the scissors
Awareness of the difficult nature of the material, texture, and size
Provided the opportunity for a collective effort and shared exposure to social judgment

Goal Fixation
Did not insist on the task being completed by the participant alone

The Surprise

Scenario

How can an individual with a developmental disability be served best when faced with unexpected obstacles that can cause agitation and insecurity?

Applying Emotional Language

I was accompanying my client on a guided tour at a facility for individuals with developmental disabilities because we were considering her possible placement there. Two officials were touring with us to answer our questions about the facility. As we approached the activity building, the front door, which was about a hundred feet away, opened and a man came out walking in our direction. We were behind the two officials, and by appearance, my client looked disinterested and unfocused. She showed no signs of anxiety, so one could assume that she was unaffected by the entrance of the other person.

Looking closely, however, I noticed that the man's hand was slightly flailing. This unexpected behavior caused alarm in my client. She quickly leaned out of the group space, trying to give the man a wide berth. She was ready to move away from the group—to flee in another direction. Because I was able to share this moment of awareness, I leaned into her space, connecting and aligning myself physically and emotionally to provide the reassurance she needed to continue our tour without any disruption or even awareness from the officials. I did not pull my client back into formation but instead made a curved path to create a greater sense of defensive space between the man and her. I was aware of the rigidity in her body as she moved away, the sudden silence after she gasped, and the darting motion signifying her flight response. This experience could have caused the tour to come to an abrupt end. However, I used sight and hearing to my advantage.

Critical Elements:

Observation
Looked at and listened to all the details of the environment

Tracking
Heard the intake of air and the sudden absence of breathing
Felt the rigidity of her body leaning back
Noticed her movement out of the group space

Sensitivity
Detected the subtle, flailing hands early
Recognized her awareness of the flailing motion

Critical Response Time
Responded quickly to her changing emotional expressions

Distance and Empathy
Evaluated the situational change from my client's perspective
Allowed her to move out of the group by widening her path

Distraction
Alert to officials' obstruction of the approaching individual

The Test

Scenario
How can a self-conscious teenager with a hidden disability be helped to avoid peer judgment and embarrassment?

Applying Emotional Language
I developed and supervised a fitness program for teens that required both physical and written tests to complete the program. All those enrolled had completed the physical skill test without a glitch. On the day of the written test, I watched the teens as they approached the test room. I noticed that one girl plodded slowly, lagging behind the others. As she entered the room, her body stiffened and she engaged in a verbal altercation with another teen.

I had not noticed this behavior from her at any point throughout the six-week program. She selected a seat in the back row but within close proximity to the other teens who were all laughing and talking. I sensed that something about the test was bothering her, but I did not want to single her out or expose her concerns to the group. Instead, I asked that all the desks be separated far apart. I passed out the tests and observed that everyone began working except for her; she just held her pencil, pretending to contemplate her answers. I moved around the room randomly asking questions of everyone with the goal of talking to her without drawing attention to her. When I reached her, I leaned in and asked if she was having any trouble reading the test. After hesitating, the answer was, "Yes." Quietly I told her I would happily accept her verbal answers. We worked together unobtrusively.

To notice her behavior was to understand that she was showing signs of growing insecurity. Along with the altercation, her body stiffened, signifying her reluctance to enter the room. To succeed, she needed help that would not compromise her self-confidence and self-esteem. I was able to remove social judgment, give her space, and earn her trust. This potentially humiliating experience became a positive one for the teen who was spared the embarrassment of addressing her reading challenge in front of her peers.

Critical Elements:

Distance and Empathy
> Felt her social pressure and understood her desire to conceal her learning disability

Observation
> Restricted physical movement indicated by her reluctance to enter the room
>
> Lack of desire to participate was inconsistent with her previous efforts

Tracking
> Noticed a change in speed in her physical movements
>
> Deterioration of her pro-social behavior

Sensitivity
> Removed exposure to social judgment by rearranging seating and talking with her privately

Goal Fixation
> Provided an alternative to standard test-taking procedure
>
> Allowed her to remain in the group and complete the goal of taking the test to the best of her ability

A Relaxed State

The power of a relaxed state is what made it possible for me to effectively utilize Emotional Language in these examples. Because experiences affecting an individual's security or insecurity come without warning, a relaxed mental and physical state is crucial. Uncommitted focus, as I shared earlier, is what allows you to capture the opportune moment and respond dynamically. When you are not drawn in by distractions or calculations, your mind and body remain more receptive to new information, allowing you to become more perceptive to emotional expressions.

Getting Started

Everyone has the foundation required to understand and use Emotional Language. If you can hear, see, smell, and touch with the slightest degree of awareness and intention, then you have what you need to begin. It is not a foreign language to any of us. In fact, this is everyone's first true language. Verbal language allows for the exchange of abstract ideas and information. It allows us to ask and answer the how and why questions of the past and the future. Emotional Language allows us to understand the present, the "now." Even the past and the future must be understood in relation to the present. Unless you address the need and meaning of the present, the past loses importance and the future loses relevancy.

Remember, the first step towards becoming fluent in Emotional Language is a profound familiarity with all of your senses. To that end, I have included an assortment of activities and suggestions for ways to enhance your sensory awareness so that you become more perceptive, thereby optimizing your ability to effectively communicate with others. Please challenge yourself with these, and add to them as well; however, use your own judgment in determining which of these activities are safe and appropriate for you.

Sensory Awareness "Workout Activities"

Look to Notice
- Open your eyes widely. You will increase peripheral vision and allow maximum access to available visual information.
- Enjoy visual art. Art captures the human emotional experience visually.
- Use rimless frames or contact lenses to cut out blind spots and increase peripheral vision.
- Minimize the use of sunglasses or tinted prescription lenses. The tint obscures subtle color changes of the skin and makes it difficult to see muscle contractions. It prevents the person with whom you are communicating from knowing your mental focus and physical alignment.
- Be aware of distractions, but do not block them. Blocking requires energy and creates blind spots. Just make a mental note of the distraction.
- Play games that require keen visual awareness.
- Play games that are safe, but use only one eye.
- Walk around in a safe place with your eyes closed.
- Look for creatures in your environment.

Hear to Discern
- Tune into a specific sound, allowing all others to move to the background.
- Minimize the use of headphones because they block other sounds from your environment.
- Converse in a whisper.
- Converse in total darkness.
- Control your need to speak.
- Listen with your eyes closed.
- Listen to the sounds in your body. If safe, use earplugs (to shut out all other sounds) when exercising.
- Listen for the depth of breath during a conversation.
- Listen for sounds that create visual images, like the wind or the ocean.
- Listen to barely audible sounds.

emotional language

- Listen to foreign languages through music or conversation. Foreign languages have sounds, pauses, tones, and pitches that are absent in your native language.
- Listen to songs. Songs provide a very deep and intimate access to the human experience of love and suffering. They capture and express emotions that are impossible to describe. You don't have to understand the lyrics if the song is in a different language. Just listen.
- Learn a new language. Although predefined structures and meanings of sound are part of any verbal language, the way in which sounds are carved out and arranged will allow you to notice the pressure points of emotional expressions when someone is speaking. Because one language does not contain all the possible tonal variations, learning different languages provides that access and listening capability.
- Listen for creatures in your environment.

Touch to Feel
- Anticipate movement: place one hand on a partner's back, and anticipate the direction in which the person will move.
- Walk holding hands with someone else without leading.
- Walk barefoot.
- Put a tiny pebble in your shoe while walking.
- Use your feet and toes to move items.
- Locate an object by feel.
- Touch as many unusual objects as possible.
- Pet an animal without disruption or distraction.
- Guide an animal without physical force.

Smell to Sense
- Identify food by smell.
- Familiarize yourself with an individual's odor.
- Identify and distinguish between healthy and unhealthy odor.
- Spend time in environments where odors are strong (gym, butchers, gardens, ethnic markets, etc.).

Expand your Practice

- Identify the point at which you become aware of a particular emotional expression.
- Stop during an activity and ask yourself which of the response systems are in motion.
- Ask yourself the following questions: How did it sound? What did it feel like? How did it smell? What did it look like? Peel back the layers of each of your senses.
- Perform an ordinary task from a different perspective.
- Take a trip or perform a task without any plan. Be spontaneous.
- Expose each of your senses in isolation to different environments. Overwhelm them and refine their awareness. Go to the extremes of your ability.
- Integrate your senses to perform a task.
- Isolate your senses to perform a task.
- Practice doing one task at a time; multi-tasking is overrated and actually decreases efficiency.
- Rely completely on another to perform a task.
- Interact with people of different races, ages, and conditions. Stay until you become comfortable and familiar and no longer feel alone.
- Avoid measuring accomplishments.
- Experience failure.
- Take a different route home each day.
- Spend time alone.
- Volunteer to rehabilitate, adopt, or provide temporary foster care for an animal. Animals that have been abused or neglected give you an unparalleled opportunity to understand and improve how you affect others.
- Practice being relaxed. Relaxation is your optimum physical and mental state. Once you have become impervious to social judgment, you will have conditioned a relaxed response.
- Be available. Actively remove mental and physical barriers that make it hard for others to get your attention and keep your interest.

What are your next steps towards Emotional Language fluency?

_____

_____

_____

_____

_____

_____

_____

_____

_____

_____

_____

_____

_____

_____

_____

_____

The Turtle and the Dog

Extend your practice into nature; walk in the garden or park or observe the plants in your house that sit alone by the window. Pay attention to what your pet is telling you by how it moves or does not, where it goes, and how it smells. Become involved with trees and animals as they are and not as how you would like them to be. Notice how each and every environmental change affects nature and animals. I am always intrigued to see how much movement there is in a tree, even when it appears not to be moving. Learning to notice movement, smell, and contrast in nature is enjoyable and reveals how much is actually going on around us that goes unnoticed.

The turtle and the dog are two animals that help us to become aware of emotional expressions. The turtle has a hard shell with a soft and vulnerable interior. When it is content, it is silent as it bathes in the sun in full view of everyone. The extension of its vulnerable body parts is always in proportion to its sense of security. The turtle retracts its head, neck, legs, and tail when it is surprised, and it hides by diving into the depths of the protective dark water below.

The dog flies the flag of peace by wagging its tail even when it barks. Its love is eternally unconditional. It bows to the rising sun to start the day or when it wants you to play. Being gregarious, it prefers to be with people than to be alone in a forest. It guards against intruders but welcomes anyone who wants to be a friend. It moves its ears in the direction of sound; it feels everything with its tongue; and it bites with its powerful jaws and sharp teeth when it has to defend. It drools uncontrollably when it smells a treat, and it stands still with a raised back when detecting hidden intensions of malice.

The turtle and the dog notice every aspect of their environment. Whether they are in clear daylight or in the darkness of night, they are both initially non-confrontational. They would rather be at peace and play than hide or bite. The relationship to their world is first one of harmony. Given the chance, I believe we are all a bit like the turtle and the dog. Our relationship with the earth, wind, fire, and water defines our relationship with each other. By taking a closer look, feel, listen, smell, and taste of our natural world, we can better understand our place in it.

Concluding Thoughts

Taking the guesswork out of any process increases our chances of success. Emotional Language takes the guesswork out of communication. It becomes particularly important when we are communicating with someone who, for whatever reason, will not or cannot verbally communicate.

When the notion of language and communication is restricted or confined to a conventionalized system of sounds, symbols, mechanical methods of exchange, and manufactured social constraints, then what we are able to experience, understand, and express becomes very limited indeed. We, in essence, sacrifice being unique sensory individuals with multifaceted and dynamic emotional needs. When our emotional needs are not met, our quality of life begins to suffer. The more we try to replace or displace emotional connections with each other and the natural world in which we live, the more vulnerable we become to mental discontentment and physical ailment. This vulnerability influences not only our immediate experience but also our long term well-being and capacity for authentic social interactions.

Throughout the years, my professional and personal life experiences have confirmed to me that we all need Emotional Language to meaningfully understand and support one another. Its significance in our lives and interpersonal communication is not a matter of opinion; it is based on our biological needs and processes as human beings.

References

Brown, Jr., T. (1983). *Tom Brown's Field Guide: Nature Observation and Tracking*. New York: Berkeley Books.

Capra, F. (1996). *The Web of Life: A New Scientific Understanding of Living Systems*. New York: Doubleday.

De Waal, F. (2005). *Our Inner Ape*. New York: Riverhead Books.

Grossman, D. (1995). *On Killing: The Psychological Cost of Learning to Kill in War and Society*. New York: Back Bay Books.

Habets, B. *How to Talk to Your Dog*. Kent, England: The Windsor Group.

Hert, R. (2007). *The Scent of Desire*. New York: HarperCollins.

Mills, K. C. (2005). *Disciplined Attention: How to Improve Your Visual Attention When You Drive*. Chapel Hill: Profile Press.

Morris, D. (1978). *Manwatching: A Field Guide to Human Behavior*. London, England: Triad/Panther Books.

Navarro, J. (2008). *What Every Body is Saying: An Ex-FBI Agent's Guide to Speed-Reading People*. New York: HarperCollins.

Sears, W.G., & Winwood, R.S. (1974). *Anatomy and Physiology for Nurses and Students of Human Biology*. London, England: Edward Arnold (Publishers) Ltd.

Weston, T. (1990). *Atlas of Anatomy*. London, England: Marshall Cavendish Books Limited

About the Author

Zaki Huq has worked in the human services profession for over thirty years. In the United Kingdom, he worked for one of Europe's largest advocacy agencies for seniors, as well as for Adult Probation Services. As a Service Development Officer he designed and implemented organizational change for increased service accessibility and integration into ethnic communities.

Across the United States, he has worked with a variety of governmental and non-profit organizations serving homeless families, gang youth, and individuals with disabilities, including Juvenile Detention and Probation Services, Child Protective Services, the YMCA, and Tribal Governments.

Throughout his career, Mr. Huq has been respected for his skill in frontline service delivery as well as preventative program design and management, both in urban and rural environments. He has a sustained commitment to increased understanding and collaboration between diverse socioeconomic and cultural groups. Living and travelling extensively in various parts of the world has given him a global perspective on communication and how it influences individuals and society.

Presently, he consults with organizations, governmental agencies, and families on approaches for integrating Emotional Language into daily communication.

Emotional Language Consulting
emotionallanguage.org

7966099R0

Made in the USA
Charleston, SC
26 April 2011